COMPONENTS OF EVANGELISM

SESSION 3

INTERFACING EVANGELISM and DISCIPLESHIP

DR. AARON R. JONES
Foreword by Dr. Timothy M. Hill

Interfacing Evangelism and Discipleship

WORKBOOK

Components of Evangelism

Dr. Aaron R. Jones

Components of Evangelism

Copyright © 2018 by Dr. Aaron R. Jones

Printed in the United States of America

Published by Kingdom Publishing, LLC, Odenton, MD 21113

All rights reserved. No part of this book may be reproduced or transmitted in any form or by any means, electronic or mechanical, including photocopying, recording or by any information storage and retrieval system without written permission from the author, except for the inclusion of brief quotations in a review.

All scripture quotations are from the King James Version of the Bible. Thomas Nelson Publishers, Nashville: Thomas Nelson, Inc. 1972

Editor: Sharon D. Jones

Graphic Designer: Janell McIlwain – JM Virtual Concepts

                Tiara Smith

ISBN 978-1-947741-18-8

Table of Contents

Interfacing Evangelism and Discipleship Sessions 1

Foreword 2

The Mission 3

The Commandment 6

The G.O.S.P.E.L 9

The Requirement (DCB) 11

The Romans Road 14

The Heart 17

The Power 20

The Increase 22

The Facts 24

The Keys 28

Works Cited 32

About the Author 33

Contact Page 34

Interfacing Evangelism and Discipleship

SESSIONS

Session 1—**Introduction and Philosophy**

Session 2—**5 Principles to Encourage Evangelism**

Session 3—**Components of Evangelism**

Session 4—**Bait for Evangelism**

Session 5—**Methodology of Evangelism**

Session 6—**Church Planting Produces Evangelism and Discipleship**

Session 7—**Babes in Christ**

Session 8—**Components of Discipleship**

Session 9—**Evangelism and Discipleship Plan**

Session 10—**Spirit of Forgiveness**

Foreword

When God calls a man of faith and fortitude to a specific purpose in the building of His Kingdom, He uses an individual like Dr. Aaron Jones.

Feeling the urgency of the hour, Dr. Jones has shaped his participation in the FINISH Commitment by emphasizing the merging of evangelism and discipleship strategies to assist churches and individuals in their quests to effectively reach the lost. As Senior Pastor of New Hope Church of God, he is well-aware of what it takes to affect the Great Commission of our Lord.

Dr. Jones' desire is to instruct others on how to deliberately make an impact on winning souls and then discipling them for powerful Christian service. His all-inclusive approach will intrigue and provide the impetus for those willing to pursue the heart of God.

Interfacing Evangelism and Discipleship will change the course of your outreach!

Dr. Timothy M. Hill
General Overseer
Church of God, Cleveland, Tennessee

The Mission

The Mission[1]

- The Great Commission is the mission of the Church.

- A Church success must be measured by the obedience and consistency to the Great Commission.

Interfacing Evangelism and Discipleship – Components of Evangelism

- We are all called to evangelize.

    _____

    _____

- We are called to seek the unsaved and unchurched.

    _____

    _____

- We must be intentional.

    _____

    _____

The Mission
Additional Notes

The Commandment

The Commandment

- What is Evangelism?

_____
_____

- Why do we need Evangelism?

_____
_____
_____

The Commandment

- What is Pre-Evangelism?

Additional Notes

The G.O.S.P.E.L

The Gospel

G_____

O_____

S_____

P_____

E_____

L_____

Additional Notes

The Requirement (DCB)

A Decision

_____
_____
_____
_____
_____

Interfacing Evangelism and Discipleship – Components of Evangelism

A Confession

_____

_____

_____

_____

_____

A Belief

_____

_____

_____

_____

_____

The Requirement (DCB)

Additional Notes

The Romans Road

The Romans Road

APLS (All, Penalty, Love, and Salvation)

- Road #1—All Are Sinners and in Need of a Savior. (Romans 3:23)

_____

_____

_____

The Romans Road

- Road #2—The Penalty of Sin is Death. (Romans 6:23)

_____

_____

_____

_____

- Road #3—Jesus' Expression of Love was to Die for our Sins. (Romans 5:8)

_____

_____

_____

_____

- Road #4—Salvation Comes Through a Confession and a Belief of Jesus' Work on the Cross. (Romans 10:9, 10)

_____

_____

_____

_____

Additional Notes

The Heart

The Heart[2]

II Peter 3:9

"The Lord is not slack concerning his promise, as some men count slackness; but is longsuffering to us-ward, not willing that any should perish, but that all should come to repentance."

_____
_____
_____
_____

I Timothy 2:4

"Who will have all men to be saved, and to come unto the knowledge of the truth."

_____

_____

_____

_____

_____

Additional Notes

The Power

The Power

"But ye shall receive power, after that the Holy Ghost is come upon you: and ye shall be witnesses unto me both in Jerusalem, and in all Judaea, and in Samaria, and unto the uttermost part of the earth." Acts 1:8

_____
_____
_____
_____
_____

Additional Notes

❖❖❖❖❖

The Increase

The Increase

"I have planted, Apollos watered; but God gave the increase." I Corinthians 3:6

_____
_____
_____
_____
_____
_____

The Increase

Additional Notes

The Facts

The Facts[3]

- No boundaries

_____

_____

- No respect of person

_____

_____

The Facts

- Involves the teaching of the Gospel

_____

_____

- Must be led by the Holy Spirit

_____

_____

- Must be done in your community

_____

_____

- Brings repentance

_____

_____

- Involves preaching and teaching

_____

_____

- Limited to one message, but different methods

_____

_____

Interfacing Evangelism and Discipleship – Components of Evangelism

- Involves being active

___

___

- Involves a promise from Jesus Christ

___

___

The Facts

Additional Notes

The Keys

The Eight Keys[4]

Express Compassion (Jude 22)

_____
_____
_____

The Keys

Know to Listen (James 1:19)

_____

_____

_____

Understand the Mindset of the Unbeliever (Romans 12:20

_____

_____

_____

Be Ready (I Peter 3:15)

_____

_____

_____

Avoid Confrontation Conversation (Titus 3:9)

_____

_____

_____

Interfacing Evangelism and Discipleship – Components of Evangelism

Observe Body Gestures and Countenances (Genesis 4:6)

_____

_____

_____

Never Say "The Bible Says" Unless You Know and Can Quote the Scripture (II Timothy 2:15)

_____

_____

_____

Adjust for Individuality (Genesis 1:26)

_____

_____

_____

Additional Notes

Works Cited

[1]Jones, Aaron R., Equipping the Church for the Harvest. (Cheltenham: Anointed Press Publishing), 2009.

[2]Jones, Aaron R., Equipping the Church for the Harvest. (Cheltenham: Anointed Press Publishing), 2009.

[3]Jones, Aaron R., Equipping the Church for the Harvest. (Cheltenham: Anointed Press Publishing), 2009.

[4]Jones, Aaron R., Eight Effective Keys to Evangelism. (Cheltenham: Anointed Press Publishing), 2003.

"Interfacing Evangelism and Discipleship to Build the Kingdom of God"

About the Author

DR. AARON R. JONES serves as Senior Pastor of New Hope Church of God. Under his pastorate is New Hope Kiddie Kollege, Inc (Daycare) and New Hope Community Outreach Services, Inc. Dr. Jones also oversees New Hope Church of God Ghana (2 churches) and New Hope Church of God Uganda (3 churches).

Dr. Jones is an Ordained Bishop with the Church of God denomination and is the DELMARVA-DC District Overseer (16 churches). Dr. Jones serves on DELMARVA-DC's Regional Council, Ministerial Internship Program Board, Urban Ministry Committee, Finance Committee, and Chaplain's Board. He also serves on both the Church of God's International and DELMARVA-DC Ministry to the Military Board. In his local community, Dr. Jones serves as a Chaplain for the Charles County Sheriff Department. He also serves as Board Secretary for the United Ministers Coalition of Southern Maryland, Inc.

Being obedient to 2 Timothy 2:15, "Study to show thyself approved...," Dr. Jones received a Doctorate in Theology and Pastoral Counseling from Life

Christian University and a Doctorate in Christian Counseling from American Christian College and Seminary. He is a certified Pastoral Counselor with the International Association of Christian Counseling Professionals. He is a Life and Pastoral Coach. He is the former Executive Vice President of the National Bible College and Seminary in Fort Washington, Maryland.

Dr. Jones has published ten books and a soul-wining project that provide a biblical foundation for Christian doctrine and discipline. He has recorded a CD entitled, Peace in the Storm. He is the founder and owner of God's Comfort Ministries, LLC, which provides Christian literature, evangelism training, and spiritual guidance. He has appeared live on TCT Network; WATC-TV's Atlanta Live; Babbie's House (hosted by CCM artist Babbie Mason); and In Concert Today on DCTV. He has done radio interviews with Radio One's WYCB's program; The Praise Fest Show; and online with Total Prayze. He was featured on the cover of Change Gospel Magazine and interviewed on Promoting Purpose Magazine.

Dr. Jones not only serves God, but his country as well. He has served over 20 years in the Armed Forces. He is a retired Chaplain with the Army National Guard. He participated in both Operation Noble Eagle (2003) and Operation Iraqi Freedom III (2005).

Dr. Jones is happily married to the former Sharon Russell. He sincerely believes without her love, support, and encouragement, many of his goals would not have been accomplished.

Contact Page

Mailing Address:

150 Post Office Road #1079

Waldorf, Maryland 20604

Website: www.godscomfort.net

Email: drjones@godscomfortmin.net

Facebook: God's Comfort Ministries

Twitter: @GodsComfort_Min

Instagram: @godscomfort_min

GOD'S COMFORT MINISTRIES

God's Comfort Ministries (GCM) provides practical Christian books, teachings, trainings, and coaching to new converts and seasoned believers. GCM provides understanding of the doctrinal principles of the Bible.

Services Provided

Pastoral and Life Coaching

Evangelism and Discipleship Training

Spiritual Guidance

New Author Consultation

Christian Literature

www.ingramcontent.com/pod-product-compliance
Lightning Source LLC
Chambersburg PA
CBHW081357080526
44588CB00016B/2527